The Soccer Training Journal: The Player's

Special Thanks

God for His graces and the opportunity to play soccer and coach.

Dave Barlow for taking this book to publication, inspiration to believe in the unbelievable, and incredible opportunities to use my abilities.

Dr. Paul Wright for encouraging me to motivate others around the world.

The DiCicco family for welcoming me to be a part of the SoccerPlus family.

Drew DiCicco, Nicholas DiCicco, and Heath Creager for being sources of motivational energy, inspiration, and mentorship.

Jeff Parrish for providing outreach to so many around the world giving me the opportunity to provide outreach and play soccer in Kenya.

Davis Ouma for inspiring my efforts to help others by being the single-most giving person that I have ever met.

Megan for being my best friend and always encouraging me in my life projects.

My parents for giving me life and the opportunity to develop as a soccer player and human being.

My extended family and friends for supporting my efforts on and off of the soccer field.

All of my many coaches throughout my life for giving me the tools to be a great player and coach by reflecting your example in my life.

My players for all of the time we have shared, your hard work, the responsibility to help develop your abilities in soccer and life, and for believing in me to make you the best player you can be.

The Soccer Training Journal

Name: _____

Birth Date: _____

City, State of Residence: _____

_____

League/Division: _____

Age: _____

Height: _____

Weight: _____

Starting Date: _____

The Soccer Training Journal: The Player's Guide to Daily Excellence

Are you a soccer coach, trainer, parent raising the next Cristiano Ronaldo, or competitive player?

This journal is for the soccer player that is serious about improving their game. The pages that follow are designed to keep the player accountable to their goals and maintain their desire for purposeful training over the course of the soccer season. By following the simple fill-in-the-blank method of this journal, the player reflects on how their actions for that day brought them closer to their soccer goals (or how their actions for that day may have detracted from their soccer goals). Drawing on experience as a player for the last 20 years, an intense interest in what allows a person to unlock the success that oftentimes lies dormant within, education in Human Performance, founding and operating a soccer club, and working with coaches from and playing soccer all over the world, it is my desire to help form the whole player by bringing awareness to the important aspects of the game by way of the skeleton provided.

Whether you are a coach looking to track your players training over the off-season, a trainer looking to keep your players honest to their soccer homework, a parent supporting your favorite player's (or players') training efforts, or that player who wants to take their game to the next level, this book is your answer!

For further resources on how to improve as a player, visit www.playbeautifulsoccer.net and www.docide.com.

The Soccer Training Journal: The Player's Guide to Daily Excellence

Description of Terms

Life Goal in Soccer: What is the highest achievement you will attain in soccer?

Season Goal in Soccer: What will you accomplish this season as an individual? As a team?

Favorite Player(s): Find a player specific to your liking. Look at players of all levels, in all positions. Find a player possesses traits that you wish to attain through working on who you are as a player and a person. You may choose to select multiple players as your favorite, selecting one for their ability to dribble at pace, another for their confidence in rallying their team when they are down, and another yet for their ability to strike the ball to hit the back of the net.

Favorite Skill(s): What is the greatest skill you have seen a player do with the ball? Think about dribbling skills, volleying skills, feints/fakes, or anything great that occurs when a player and a soccer ball combine.

Best Personal Soccer Attribute(s): What do you do best in soccer? What is your signature trait? Are you the team motivator? The freekicker? The goalkeeper that never cracks under pressure? What makes you special in the game of soccer? What do you contribute to your team?

Physical Game: Did you get touches on the ball? Train strikes on goal? Perform interval running? Strength training? Provide a detailed record of the physical components of soccer that you trained.

Psychological/Mental Game: Did you visualize yourself being successful on the soccer field as you went to sleep? Did you listen to a motivational speech? Did you use positive self-affirmations? Provide a detailed record of the psychological components of soccer that you trained.

Tactical Game: Did you play the game with others today? Did you watch the game on television or in person? Did you write out formations in your notebook and draw how players move as the ball move across the pitch? Provide a detailed record of the tactical components of soccer that you trained.

Nutrition:

    Food: What did you eat? Did you know that vitamins and minerals are essential to our body's ability to turn what we eat into fuel that our body uses to play soccer? Without adequate vitamins and minerals, which are found most abundantly in unprocessed foods such as fresh vegetables and fruits, we limit our abilities as a player. Make sure to eat fresh vegetables, fruits, and unprocessed foods to fuel your soccer performance.

    Water: What sources of fluids did you consume? How much? Did you know that the human body is approximately 68% water (Mitchell, 1945). Leaner individuals (most soccer players) have higher amounts of water in their body than less lean individuals. Your muscles, which fuel your performance on the pitch, are approximately 80% water (Mitchell, 1945). Proper hydration is vital to optimal soccer performance.

The Big Picture

Sample Page

Life Goal in Soccer: I will play professional soccer in the Kenyan Premier League for Kakamega Homeboyz F.C.

Season Goal in Soccer: I will score 5 goals and contribute 10 assists. My team will finish first place in our league.

Favorite Player(s): Ronaldinho, Zlatan, Zidane, Twellman, Roberto Carlos, Buffon

Favorite Skill(s): elastico, Akka 3000, Tsatsulow ATW, rainbow-bike, travella shot, knuckle ball shot, driven ball pass, bicycle kick, scissor kick

Best Personal Soccer Attribute(s): Crossing ability, passing, positional intelligence

The Big Picture

"In order to succeed, we must first believe that we can."-Nikos Kazantzakis

Life Goal in Soccer: _____

_____

Season Goal in Soccer: _____

_____

Favorite Player(s): _____

_____

_____

Favorite Skill(s): _____

_____

_____

Best Personal Soccer Attribute(s): _____

_____

The Soccer Training Journal: The Player's Guide to Daily Excellence

Day 1: The Journey begins

Sample Page

Time Invested **Component** **What you did**

60 min. **Physical Game:** 100 juggles per foot, 50 shots on goal, 20 dribbles at top speed for 20 yards each

10 min. **Psychological/Mental Game:** I watched a video of Neymar beating defenders in games then visualized myself doing these skills in my next game.

30 min. **Tactical Game:** I scrimmaged 3v3 with my friends in my back yard.

Nutrition

Food: Breakfast: pancakes and eggs   Snack: granola bar
Lunch: apple, turkey sandwich   Snack: pretzels
Dinner: spaghetti with meatballs   Dessert: yogurt

Water: I drank 8 cups of water today; two cups with each meal and one with each snack. I drank gatorade after training.

What did you learn today? I learned the elastico move.

Did you accomplish your goal today? Yes, I got 10 left-footed juggles in-a-row.

What is your goal for tomorrow? I will take 55 shots on goal.

Additional Notes: I scored the game-winning goal with my left foot in 3v3.

Running Totals: Physical- 1 hour   Mental/Psychological- 10 min.   Tactical- 30 min.

The Soccer Training Journal: The Player's Guide to Daily Excellence

Day 1: The Journey begins

"What you do today can improve all of your tomorrows." -Ralph Marston

<u>Time Invested</u>   <u>Component</u>   <u>What you did</u>

Physical Game: _____

_____

_____

Psychological/Mental Game: _____

_____

_____

Tactical Game: _____

_____

_____

Nutrition

Food: _____

_____

_____

Water: _____

_____

What did you learn today? _____

_____

Did you accomplish your goal today? _____

_____

What is your goal for tomorrow? _____

_____

Additional Notes: _____

Running Totals: Physical-   Mental/Psychological-   Tactical-

Day 2

"Always do your best. What you plant now, you will harvest later." -Og Mandino

<u>Time Invested</u> <u>Component</u> <u>What you did</u>

        Physical Game: _____

_____

_____

        Psychological/Mental Game: _____

_____

_____

        Tactical Game: _____

_____

_____

Nutrition

Food: _____

_____

_____

Water: _____

_____

What did you learn today? _____

_____

Did you accomplish your goal today? _____

_____

What is your goal for tomorrow? _____

_____

Additional Notes: _____

Running Totals: Physical-   Mental/Psychological-   Tactical-

Day 3

"With the new day comes new strength and new thoughts." -Eleanor Roosevelt

<u>Time Invested</u>   <u>Component</u>   <u>What you did</u>

Physical Game: _____

_____

_____

Psychological/Mental Game: _____

_____

_____

Tactical Game: _____

_____

_____

Nutrition

Food: _____

_____

_____

Water: _____

_____

What did you learn today? _____

_____

Did you accomplish your goal today? _____

_____

What is your goal for tomorrow? _____

_____

Additional Notes: _____

Running Totals: Physical-   Mental/Psychological-   Tactical-

The Soccer Training Journal: The Player's Guide to Daily Excellence

Day 4

"The most certain way to succeed is always to try just one more time." -Thomas A. Edison

<u>Time Invested</u> <u>Component</u> <u>What you did</u>

       Physical Game: _____

_____

_____

       Psychological/Mental Game: _____

_____

_____

       Tactical Game: _____

_____

_____

Nutrition

Food: _____

_____

_____

Water: _____

_____

What did you learn today? _____

_____

Did you accomplish your goal today? _____

_____

What is your goal for tomorrow? _____

_____

Additional Notes: _____

Running Totals: Physical-   Mental/Psychological-   Tactical-

The Soccer Training Journal: The Player's Guide to Daily Excellence

Day 5

"You can't cross the sea merely by standing and staring at the water." -Rabindranath Tagore

<u>Time Invested</u>   <u>Component</u>   <u>What you did</u>

   Physical Game: _____

_____

_____

   Psychological/Mental Game: _____

_____

_____

   Tactical Game: _____

_____

_____

Nutrition

Food: _____

_____

_____

Water: _____

_____

What did you learn today? _____

_____

Did you accomplish your goal today? _____

_____

What is your goal for tomorrow? _____

_____

Additional Notes: _____

Running Totals: Physical- Mental/Psychological- Tactical-

The Soccer Training Journal: The Player's Guide to Daily Excellence

Day 6

"Nothing can be done without hope and confidence."-Helen Keller

Time Invested   Component   What you did

Physical Game: _____

_____

_____

Psychological/Mental Game: _____

_____

_____

Tactical Game: _____

_____

_____

Nutrition

Food: _____

_____

_____

Water: _____

_____

What did you learn today? _____

_____

Did you accomplish your goal today? _____

_____

What is your goal for tomorrow? _____

_____

Additional Notes: _____

Running Totals: Physical-   Mental/Psychological-   Tactical-

The Soccer Training Journal: The Player's Guide to Daily Excellence

Day 7

"The best preparation for tomorrow is doing your best today." -H. Jackson Brown, Jr.

<u>Time Invested</u> <u>Component</u> <u>What you did</u>

Physical Game: _____

_____

_____

Psychological/Mental Game: _____

_____

_____

Tactical Game: _____

_____

_____

Nutrition

Food: _____

_____

_____

Water: _____

_____

What did you learn today? _____

_____

Did you accomplish your goal today? _____

_____

What is your goal for tomorrow? _____

_____

Additional Notes: _____

Running Totals: Physical-   Mental/Psychological-   Tactical-

The Soccer Training Journal: The Player's Guide to Daily Excellence

Day 8

"Start by doing what's necessary; then do what's possible; and suddenly you are doing the impossible."-St. Francis of Assisi

<u>Time Invested</u>　<u>Component</u>　<u>What you did</u>

Physical Game: _____

_____

_____

Psychological/Mental Game: _____

_____

_____

Tactical Game: _____

_____

_____

Nutrition

Food: _____

_____

_____

Water: _____

_____

What did you learn today? _____

_____

Did you accomplish your goal today? _____

_____

What is your goal for tomorrow? _____

_____

Additional Notes: _____

Running Totals:　　Physical-　　Mental/Psychological-　　Tactical-

Day 9

"What we think, we become." -Buddha

<u>Time Invested</u> <u>Component</u> <u>What you did</u>

        Physical Game: _____

_____

_____

        Psychological/Mental Game: _____

_____

_____

        Tactical Game: _____

_____

_____

Nutrition

Food: _____

_____

_____

Water: _____

_____

What did you learn today? _____

_____

Did you accomplish your goal today? _____

_____

What is your goal for tomorrow? _____

_____

Additional Notes: _____

Running Totals: Physical-   Mental/Psychological-   Tactical-

The Soccer Training Journal: The Player's Guide to Daily Excellence

Day 10

"Change your thoughts and change your world." -Norman Vincent Peale

<u>Time Invested</u> <u>Component</u> <u>What you did</u>

    Physical Game: _____

_____

_____

    Psychological/Mental Game: _____

_____

_____

    Tactical Game: _____

_____

_____

Nutrition

Food: _____

_____

_____

Water: _____

_____

What did you learn today? _____

_____

Did you accomplish your goal today? _____

_____

What is your goal for tomorrow? _____

_____

Additional Notes: _____

Running Totals: Physical-   Mental/Psychological-   Tactical-

The Soccer Training Journal: The Player's Guide to Daily Excellence

Day 11

"Put your heart, mind, and soul into even your smallest acts. This is the secret of success." -Swami Sivananda

<u>Time Invested</u>   <u>Component</u>   <u>What you did</u>

Physical Game: _____

_____

_____

Psychological/Mental Game: _____

_____

_____

Tactical Game: _____

_____

_____

Nutrition

Food: _____

_____

_____

Water: _____

_____

What did you learn today? _____

_____

Did you accomplish your goal today? _____

_____

What is your goal for tomorrow? _____

_____

Additional Notes: _____

Running Totals: Physical-   Mental/Psychological-   Tactical-

The Soccer Training Journal: The Player's Guide to Daily Excellence

Day 12

"If opportunity doesn't knock, build a door." -Milton Berle

Time Invested Component What you did

    Physical Game: _____

_____

_____

    Psychological/Mental Game: _____

_____

_____

    Tactical Game: _____

_____

_____

Nutrition

Food: _____

_____

_____

Water: _____

_____

What did you learn today? _____

_____

Did you accomplish your goal today? _____

_____

What is your goal for tomorrow? _____

_____

Additional Notes: _____

Running Totals: Physical-   Mental/Psychological-   Tactical-

The Soccer Training Journal: The Player's Guide to Daily Excellence

Day 13

"The measure of who we are is what we do with what we have." -Vince Lombardi

<u>Time Invested</u>   <u>Component</u>   <u>What you did</u>

      Physical Game: _____

_____

_____

      Psychological/Mental Game: _____

_____

_____

      Tactical Game: _____

_____

_____

Nutrition

Food: _____

_____

_____

Water: _____

_____

What did you learn today? _____

_____

Did you accomplish your goal today? _____

_____

What is your goal for tomorrow? _____

_____

Additional Notes: _____

Running Totals: Physical-   Mental/Psychological-   Tactical-

The Soccer Training Journal: The Player's Guide to Daily Excellence

Day 14

"Somewhere, something incredible is waiting to be known." -Carl Sagan

Time Invested   Component   What you did

        Physical Game: _____

_____

_____

        Psychological/Mental Game: _____

_____

_____

        Tactical Game: _____

_____

_____

Nutrition

Food: _____

_____

_____

Water: _____

_____

What did you learn today?_____

_____

Did you accomplish your goal today?_____

_____

What is your goal for tomorrow? _____

_____

Additional Notes: _____

Running Totals: Physical-   Mental/Psychological-   Tactical-

Day 15

"No matter what people tell you, words and ideas can change the world." -Robin Williams

<u>Time Invested</u>   <u>Component</u>   <u>What you did</u>

Physical Game: _____

_____

_____

Psychological/Mental Game: _____

_____

_____

Tactical Game: _____

_____

_____

Nutrition

Food: _____

_____

_____

Water: _____

_____

What did you learn today? _____

_____

Did you accomplish your goal today? _____

_____

What is your goal for tomorrow? _____

_____

Additional Notes: _____

Running Totals: Physical-   Mental/Psychological-   Tactical-

Fill This Page with Positive Personal Statements

I am a great soccer player.

I love the person that I am becoming with my hard work each and every day.

Day 16

"Happiness does not come from doing easy work but from the afterglow of satisfaction that comes after the achievement of a difficult task that demanded our best." -Theodore Isaac Rubin

<u>Time Invested</u>   <u>Component</u>   <u>What you did</u>

      Physical Game: _____

_____

_____

      Psychological/Mental Game: _____

_____

_____

      Tactical Game: _____

_____

_____

Nutrition

Food: _____

_____

_____

Water: _____

_____

What did you learn today? _____

_____

Did you accomplish your goal today? _____

_____

What is your goal for tomorrow? _____

_____

Additional Notes: _____

Running Totals: Physical-   Mental/Psychological-   Tactical-

Day 17

"Without continual growth and progress, such words as improvement, achievement, and success have no meaning."-Benjamin Franklin

<u>Time Invested</u> <u>Component</u> <u>What you did</u>

        Physical Game: _____

_____

_____

        Psychological/Mental Game: _____

_____

_____

        Tactical Game: _____

_____

_____

Nutrition

Food: _____

_____

_____

Water: _____

_____

What did you learn today? _____

_____

Did you accomplish your goal today? _____

_____

What is your goal for tomorrow? _____

_____

Additional Notes: _____

Running Totals: Physical-   Mental/Psychological-   Tactical-

The Soccer Training Journal: The Player's Guide to Daily Excellence

Day 18

"High achievement always takes place in the framework of high expectation." -Charles Kettering

<u>Time Invested</u>   <u>Component</u>   <u>What you did</u>

   Physical Game: _____

_____

_____

   Psychological/Mental Game: _____

_____

_____

   Tactical Game: _____

_____

_____

Nutrition

Food: _____

_____

_____

Water: _____

_____

What did you learn today? _____

_____

Did you accomplish your goal today? _____

_____

What is your goal for tomorrow? _____

_____

Additional Notes: _____

Running Totals: Physical- Mental/Psychological- Tactical-

The Soccer Training Journal: The Player's Guide to Daily Excellence

Day 19

"Optimism is essential to achievement, and it is also the foundation of courage and true progress."-Nicholas M. Butler

Time Invested   Component   What you did

      Physical Game: _____

_____

_____

      Psychological/Mental Game: _____

_____

_____

      Tactical Game: _____

_____

_____

Nutrition

Food: _____

_____

Water: _____

_____

What did you learn today? _____

_____

Did you accomplish your goal today? _____

_____

What is your goal for tomorrow? _____

_____

Additional Notes: _____

Running Totals: Physical-   Mental/Psychological-   Tactical-

The Soccer Training Journal: The Player's Guide to Daily Excellence

Day 20

"Don't mistake activity for achievement. Practice it the right way."-John Wooden

Time Invested   Component   What you did

      Physical Game: _____

_____

_____

      Psychological/Mental Game: _____

_____

_____

      Tactical Game: _____

_____

_____

Nutrition

Food: _____

_____

_____

Water: _____

_____

What did you learn today? _____

_____

Did you accomplish your goal today? _____

_____

What is your goal for tomorrow? _____

_____

Additional Notes: _____

Running Totals: Physical-   Mental/Psychological-   Tactical-

The Soccer Training Journal: The Player's Guide to Daily Excellence

Day 21

"You can't get much done in life if you only work on the days when you feel good." -Jerry West

<u>Time Invested</u> <u>Component</u> <u>What you did</u>

Physical Game: _____

_____

_____

Psychological/Mental Game: _____

_____

_____

Tactical Game: _____

_____

_____

Nutrition

Food: _____

_____

_____

Water: _____

_____

What did you learn today? _____

_____

Did you accomplish your goal today? _____

_____

What is your goal for tomorrow? _____

_____

Additional Notes: _____

Running Totals: Physical-   Mental/Psychological-   Tactical-

Day 22

"Things turn out best for the people who make the best of the way things turn out."-John Wooden

<u>Time Invested</u> <u>Component</u> <u>What you did</u>

    Physical Game: _____

_____

_____

    Psychological/Mental Game: _____

_____

_____

    Tactical Game: _____

_____

_____

Nutrition

Food: _____

_____

_____

Water: _____

_____

What did you learn today? _____

_____

Did you accomplish your goal today? _____

_____

What is your goal for tomorrow? _____

_____

Additional Notes: _____

Running Totals: Physical-   Mental/Psychological-   Tactical-

The Soccer Training Journal: The Player's Guide to Daily Excellence

Day 23

"If you're not making mistakes, then you're not doing anything. I'm positive that a doer makes mistakes."-John Wooden

<u>Time Invested</u> <u>Component</u> <u>What you did</u>

       Physical Game: _____

_____

_____

       Psychological/Mental Game: _____

_____

_____

       Tactical Game: _____

_____

_____

Nutrition

Food: _____

_____

_____

Water: _____

_____

What did you learn today? _____

_____

Did you accomplish your goal today? _____

_____

What is your goal for tomorrow? _____

_____

Additional Notes: _____

<u>Running Totals:</u>   Physical-   Mental/Psychological-   Tactical-

Day 24

"Weakness of attitude becomes weakness of character." -Albert Einstein

<u>Time Invested</u> <u>Component</u> <u>What you did</u>

        Physical Game: _____

_____

_____

        Psychological/Mental Game: _____

_____

_____

        Tactical Game: _____

_____

_____

Nutrition

Food: _____

_____

_____

Water: _____

_____

What did you learn today? _____

_____

Did you accomplish your goal today? _____

_____

What is your goal for tomorrow? _____

_____

Additional Notes: _____

Running Totals: Physical-   Mental/Psychological-   Tactical-

The Soccer Training Journal: The Player's Guide to Daily Excellence

Day 25

"Strength does not come from physical capacity. It comes from an indomitable will."-Mahatma Gandhi

Time Invested   Component   What you did

               Physical Game: _____

_____

_____

               Psychological/Mental Game: _____

_____

_____

               Tactical Game: _____

_____

_____

Nutrition

Food: _____

_____

_____

Water: _____

_____

What did you learn today? _____

_____

Did you accomplish your goal today? _____

_____

What is your goal for tomorrow? _____

_____

Additional Notes: _____

Running Totals: Physical-   Mental/Psychological-   Tactical-

Day 26

"When love and skill work together, expect a masterpiece." -John Ruskin

Time Invested   Component   What you did

        Physical Game: _____

_____

_____

        Psychological/Mental Game: _____

_____

_____

        Tactical Game: _____

_____

_____

Nutrition

Food: _____

_____

_____

Water: _____

_____

What did you learn today? _____

_____

Did you accomplish your goal today? _____

_____

What is your goal for tomorrow? _____

_____

Additional Notes: _____

Running Totals: Physical-   Mental/Psychological-   Tactical-

The Soccer Training Journal: The Player's Guide to Daily Excellence

Day 27

"Only those who have patience to do simple things perfectly ever acquire the skill to do difficult things easily." -James J. Corbett

<u>Time Invested</u>   <u>Component</u>   <u>What you did</u>

      Physical Game: _____

_____

_____

      Psychological/Mental Game: _____

_____

_____

      Tactical Game: _____

_____

_____

Nutrition

Food: _____

_____

_____

Water: _____

_____

What did you learn today? _____

_____

Did you accomplish your goal today? _____

_____

What is your goal for tomorrow? _____

_____

Additional Notes: _____

Running Totals: Physical-   Mental/Psychological-   Tactical-

The Soccer Training Journal: The Player's Guide to Daily Excellence

Day 28

"What we fear of doing most is usually what we most need to do." -Ralph Waldo Emerson

<u>Time Invested</u>   <u>Component</u>   <u>What you did</u>

Physical Game: _____

_____

_____

Psychological/Mental Game: _____

_____

_____

Tactical Game: _____

_____

_____

Nutrition

Food: _____

_____

_____

Water: _____

_____

What did you learn today? _____

_____

Did you accomplish your goal today? _____

_____

What is your goal for tomorrow? _____

_____

Additional Notes: _____

Running Totals: Physical-   Mental/Psychological-   Tactical-

The Soccer Training Journal: The Player's Guide to Daily Excellence

Day 29

"Know who you are, and be it. Know what you want, and go out and get it!"-Carroll Bryant

<u>Time Invested</u>   <u>Component</u>   <u>What you did</u>

       Physical Game: _____

_____

_____

       Psychological/Mental Game: _____

_____

_____

       Tactical Game: _____

_____

_____

Nutrition

Food: _____

_____

_____

Water: _____

_____

What did you learn today? _____

_____

Did you accomplish your goal today? _____

_____

What is your goal for tomorrow? _____

_____

Additional Notes: _____

Running Totals: Physical-   Mental/Psychological-   Tactical-

The Soccer Training Journal: The Player's Guide to Daily Excellence

Day 30

"To become a master at any skill, it takes the total effort of your: heart, mind, and soul working together in tandem."-Maurice Young

Time Invested   Component   What you did

Physical Game: _____

_____

_____

Psychological/Mental Game: _____

_____

_____

Tactical Game: _____

_____

_____

Nutrition

Food: _____

_____

_____

Water: _____

_____

What did you learn today? _____

_____

Did you accomplish your goal today? _____

_____

What is your goal for tomorrow? _____

_____

Additional Notes: _____

Running Totals: Physical-   Mental/Psychological-   Tactical-

The Soccer Training Journal: The Player's Guide to Daily Excellence

Fill This Page with a Drawing of What Your Success Will Look Like

Sample Page

The Soccer Training Journal: The Player's Guide to Daily Excellence

Fill This Page with a Drawing of What Your Success Will Look Like

The Soccer Training Journal: The Player's Guide to Daily Excellence

Day 31

"Any ideas, plan, or purpose may be placed in the mind through repetition of thought."-
Napoleon Hill

<u>Time Invested</u> <u>Component</u> <u>What you did</u>

      Physical Game: _____

_____

_____

      Psychological/Mental Game: _____

_____

_____

      Tactical Game: _____

_____

_____

Nutrition

Food: _____

_____

_____

Water: _____

_____

What did you learn today? _____

_____

Did you accomplish your goal today? _____

_____

What is your goal for tomorrow? _____

_____

Additional Notes: _____

Running Totals: Physical-   Mental/Psychological-   Tactical-

The Soccer Training Journal: The Player's Guide to Daily Excellence

Day 32

"We can change our own life and ultimately change the world." -Kristi Bowman

<u>Time Invested</u> <u>Component</u> <u>What you did</u>

          Physical Game: _____

_____

_____

          Psychological/Mental Game: _____

_____

_____

          Tactical Game: _____

_____

_____

Nutrition

Food: _____

_____

_____

Water: _____

_____

What did you learn today? _____

_____

Did you accomplish your goal today? _____

_____

What is your goal for tomorrow? _____

_____

Additional Notes: _____

Running Totals: Physical-   Mental/Psychological-   Tactical-

The Soccer Training Journal: The Player's Guide to Daily Excellence

Day 33

"You miss 100% of the shots you don't take."-Wayne Gretzky

<u>Time Invested</u> <u>Component</u> <u>What you did</u>

    Physical Game: _____

_____

_____

    Psychological/Mental Game: _____

_____

_____

    Tactical Game: _____

_____

_____

Nutrition

Food: _____

_____

_____

Water: _____

_____

What did you learn today? _____

_____

Did you accomplish your goal today? _____

_____

What is your goal for tomorrow? _____

_____

Additional Notes: _____

Running Totals: Physical-   Mental/Psychological-   Tactical-

Day 34

"What holds most people back isn't the quality of their ideas but their lack of faith in themselves. You have to live as if you are already where you want to be."-Russell Simmons

<u>Time Invested</u>   <u>Component</u>   <u>What you did</u>

    Physical Game: _____

_____

_____

    Psychological/Mental Game: _____

_____

_____

    Tactical Game: _____

_____

_____

Nutrition

Food: _____

_____

_____

Water: _____

_____

What did you learn today? _____

_____

Did you accomplish your goal today? _____

_____

What is your goal for tomorrow? _____

_____

Additional Notes: _____

Running Totals: Physical-   Mental/Psychological-   Tactical-

The Soccer Training Journal: The Player's Guide to Daily Excellence

Day 35

"He who is not courageous enough to take risks will accomplish nothing in life." -Muhammad Ali

<u>Time Invested</u>   <u>Component</u>   <u>What you did</u>

    Physical Game: _____

_____

_____

    Psychological/Mental Game: _____

_____

_____

    Tactical Game: _____

_____

_____

Nutrition

Food: _____

_____

_____

Water: _____

_____

What did you learn today? _____

_____

Did you accomplish your goal today? _____

_____

What is your goal for tomorrow? _____

_____

Additional Notes: _____

Running Totals: Physical-   Mental/Psychological-   Tactical-

The Soccer Training Journal: The Player's Guide to Daily Excellence

Day 36

"If you want to lead an extraordinary life, find out what the ordinary do—and don't do it."- Tommy Newberry

<u>Time Invested</u>   <u>Component</u>   <u>What you did</u>

        Physical Game: _____

_____

_____

        Psychological/Mental Game: _____

_____

_____

        Tactical Game: _____

_____

_____

Nutrition

Food: _____

_____

_____

Water: _____

_____

What did you learn today?_____

_____

Did you accomplish your goal today?_____

_____

What is your goal for tomorrow? _____

_____

Additional Notes: _____

Running Totals: Physical-   Mental/Psychological-   Tactical-

Day 37

"If you want to increase your success rate, double your failure rate." -Thomas Watson

Time Invested Component What you did

        Physical Game: _____

_____

_____

        Psychological/Mental Game: _____

_____

_____

        Tactical Game: _____

_____

_____

Nutrition

Food: _____

_____

_____

Water: _____

_____

What did you learn today? _____

_____

Did you accomplish your goal today? _____

_____

What is your goal for tomorrow? _____

_____

Additional Notes: _____

Running Totals: Physical-   Mental/Psychological-   Tactical-

The Soccer Training Journal: The Player's Guide to Daily Excellence

Day 38

"I've failed over and over and over again. And that is why I succeed." -Michael Jordan

<u>Time Invested</u>   <u>Component</u>   <u>What you did</u>

Physical Game: _____

_____

_____

Psychological/Mental Game: _____

_____

_____

Tactical Game: _____

_____

_____

Nutrition

Food: _____

_____

_____

Water: _____

_____

What did you learn today? _____

_____

Did you accomplish your goal today? _____

_____

What is your goal for tomorrow? _____

_____

Additional Notes: _____

Running Totals: Physical-   Mental/Psychological-   Tactical-

The Soccer Training Journal: The Player's Guide to Daily Excellence

Day 39

"I'd rather attempt to do something great and fail than to attempt nothing and succeed." -Robert H. Schuller

<u>Time Invested</u> <u>Component</u> <u>What you did</u>

  Physical Game: _____

_____

_____

  Psychological/Mental Game: _____

_____

_____

  Tactical Game: _____

_____

_____

Nutrition

Food: _____

_____

_____

Water: _____

_____

What did you learn today? _____

_____

Did you accomplish your goal today? _____

_____

What is your goal for tomorrow? _____

_____

Additional Notes: _____

Running Totals: Physical- Mental/Psychological- Tactical-

The Soccer Training Journal: The Player's Guide to Daily Excellence

Day 40

"Once you eliminate the impossible, whatever remains, no matter how improbable, must be the truth."-Arthur Conan Doyle

<u>Time Invested</u> <u>Component</u> <u>What you did</u>

Physical Game: _____

_____

_____

Psychological/Mental Game: _____

_____

_____

Tactical Game: _____

_____

_____

Nutrition

Food: _____

_____

_____

Water: _____

_____

What did you learn today?_____

_____

Did you accomplish your goal today?_____

_____

What is your goal for tomorrow? _____

_____

Additional Notes: _____

Running Totals: Physical-   Mental/Psychological-   Tactical-

The Soccer Training Journal: The Player's Guide to Daily Excellence

Day 41

"Genius is one percent inspiration and ninety-nine percent perspiration." -Thomas A. Edison

<u>Time Invested</u>   <u>Component</u>   <u>What you did</u>

        Physical Game: _____

_____

_____

        Psychological/Mental Game: _____

_____

_____

        Tactical Game: _____

_____

_____

Nutrition

Food: _____

_____

_____

Water: _____

_____

What did you learn today?_____

_____

Did you accomplish your goal today?_____

_____

What is your goal for tomorrow? _____

_____

Additional Notes: _____

Running Totals: Physical-   Mental/Psychological-   Tactical-

The Soccer Training Journal: The Player's Guide to Daily Excellence

Day 42

"Success is the sum of small efforts, repeated day in and day out." -Robert Collier

<u>Time Invested</u> <u>Component</u> <u>What you did</u>

      Physical Game: _____

_____

_____

      Psychological/Mental Game: _____

_____

_____

      Tactical Game: _____

_____

_____

Nutrition

Food: _____

_____

_____

Water: _____

_____

What did you learn today? _____

_____

Did you accomplish your goal today? _____

_____

What is your goal for tomorrow? _____

_____

Additional Notes: _____

Running Totals: Physical-   Mental/Psychological-   Tactical-

Day 43

"I wake up every day on purpose." -Heath Creager

<u>Time Invested</u>   <u>Component</u>   <u>What you did</u>

       Physical Game: _____

       Psychological/Mental Game: _____

       Tactical Game: _____

Nutrition

Food: _____

Water: _____

What did you learn today? _____

Did you accomplish your goal today? _____

What is your goal for tomorrow? _____

Additional Notes: _____

Running Totals: Physical-   Mental/Psychological-   Tactical-

The Soccer Training Journal: The Player's Guide to Daily Excellence

The Soccer Training Journal: The Player's Guide to Daily Excellence

Day 44

"Too many of us are not living our dreams because we are living our fears." -Les Brown

<u>Time Invested</u>   <u>Component</u>   <u>What you did</u>

Physical Game: _____

_____

_____

Psychological/Mental Game: _____

_____

_____

Tactical Game: _____

_____

_____

Nutrition

Food: _____

_____

_____

Water: _____

_____

What did you learn today? _____

_____

Did you accomplish your goal today? _____

_____

What is your goal for tomorrow? _____

_____

Additional Notes: _____

Running Totals: Physical-   Mental/Psychological-   Tactical-

Day 45

"It is your passion that empowers you to be able to do that thing you were created to do."- Bishop T.D. Jakes

<u>Time Invested</u>   <u>Component</u>   <u>What you did</u>

        Physical Game: _____

_____

_____

        Psychological/Mental Game: _____

_____

_____

        Tactical Game: _____

_____

_____

Nutrition

Food: _____

_____

_____

Water: _____

_____

What did you learn today? _____

_____

Did you accomplish your goal today? _____

_____

What is your goal for tomorrow? _____

_____

Additional Notes: _____

Running Totals: Physical-   Mental/Psychological-   Tactical-

The Soccer Training Journal: The Player's Guide to Daily Excellence

Fill This Page with Quotes That Motivate You

Day 46

"Life opens up opportunities to you, and you either take them or you stay afraid of taking them."-Jim Carrey

Time Invested Component What you did

    Physical Game: _____

_____

_____

    Psychological/Mental Game: _____

_____

_____

    Tactical Game: _____

_____

_____

Nutrition

Food: _____

_____

_____

Water: _____

_____

What did you learn today? _____

_____

Did you accomplish your goal today? _____

_____

What is your goal for tomorrow? _____

_____

Additional Notes: _____

Running Totals:　　　Physical-　　　Mental/Psychological-　　　Tactical-

The Soccer Training Journal: The Player's Guide to Daily Excellence

Day 47

"It's not about what you get, it's about who you're becoming." -Elliott Hulse

<u>Time Invested</u>   <u>Component</u>   <u>What you did</u>

      Physical Game: _____

_____

_____

      Psychological/Mental Game: _____

_____

_____

      Tactical Game: _____

_____

_____

Nutrition

Food: _____

_____

_____

Water: _____

_____

What did you learn today? _____

_____

Did you accomplish your goal today? _____

_____

What is your goal for tomorrow? _____

_____

Additional Notes: _____

Running Totals: Physical-   Mental/Psychological-   Tactical-

The Soccer Training Journal: The Player's Guide to Daily Excellence

Day 48

"When you want to succeed as bad as you want to breathe, then you'll be successful." -Eric Thomas

<u>Time Invested</u> <u>Component</u> <u>What you did</u>

Physical Game: _____

_____

_____

Psychological/Mental Game: _____

_____

_____

Tactical Game: _____

_____

_____

Nutrition

Food: _____

_____

_____

Water: _____

_____

What did you learn today? _____

_____

Did you accomplish your goal today? _____

_____

What is your goal for tomorrow? _____

_____

Additional Notes: _____

Running Totals: Physical-   Mental/Psychological-   Tactical-

The Soccer Training Journal: The Player's Guide to Daily Excellence

Day 49

"Most of you don't want success as much as you want to sleep!" -Eric Thomas

<u>Time Invested</u>   <u>Component</u>   <u>What you did</u>

        Physical Game: _____

_____

_____

        Psychological/Mental Game: _____

_____

_____

        Tactical Game: _____

_____

_____

Nutrition

Food: _____

_____

_____

Water: _____

_____

What did you learn today? _____

_____

Did you accomplish your goal today? _____

_____

What is your goal for tomorrow? _____

_____

Additional Notes: _____

Running Totals: Physical-   Mental/Psychological-   Tactical-

The Soccer Training Journal: The Player's Guide to Daily Excellence

Day 50

"Take up one idea. Make that one idea your life—think of it, dream of it, live on that idea." -Swami Vivekananda

<u>Time Invested</u> <u>Component</u> <u>What you did</u>

       Physical Game: _____

_____

_____

       Psychological/Mental Game: _____

_____

_____

       Tactical Game: _____

_____

_____

Nutrition

Food: _____

_____

_____

Water: _____

_____

What did you learn today? _____

_____

Did you accomplish your goal today? _____

_____

What is your goal for tomorrow? _____

_____

Additional Notes: _____

Running Totals: Physical-   Mental/Psychological-   Tactical-

Day 51

"You're going to go through tough times—that's life. But I say, 'Nothing happens to you, it happens for you.' See the positive in negative events."-Joel Osteen

<u>Time Invested</u> <u>Component</u> <u>What you did</u>

Physical Game: _____

_____

_____

Psychological/Mental Game: _____

_____

_____

Tactical Game: _____

_____

_____

Nutrition

Food: _____

_____

_____

Water: _____

_____

What did you learn today? _____

_____

Did you accomplish your goal today? _____

_____

What is your goal for tomorrow? _____

_____

Additional Notes: _____

Running Totals: Physical-   Mental/Psychological-   Tactical-

The Soccer Training Journal: The Player's Guide to Daily Excellence

Day 52

"We are all faced with a series of great opportunities brilliantly disguised as impossible situations."-Charles R. Swindoll

<u>Time Invested</u>   <u>Component</u>   <u>What you did</u>

      Physical Game: _____

_____

_____

      Psychological/Mental Game: _____

_____

_____

      Tactical Game: _____

_____

_____

Nutrition

Food: _____

_____

_____

Water: _____

_____

What did you learn today?_____

_____

Did you accomplish your goal today?_____

_____

What is your goal for tomorrow? _____

_____

Additional Notes: _____

Running Totals: Physical-   Mental/Psychological-   Tactical-

The Soccer Training Journal: The Player's Guide to Daily Excellence

Day 53

"Success is no accident. It is hard work, perseverance, learning, studying, sacrifice and most of all, love of what you are doing or learning to do." -Pelé

Time Invested   Component   What you did

    Physical Game: _____

_____

_____

    Psychological/Mental Game: _____

_____

_____

    Tactical Game: _____

_____

_____

Nutrition

Food: _____

_____

_____

Water: _____

_____

What did you learn today? _____

_____

Did you accomplish your goal today? _____

_____

What is your goal for tomorrow? _____

_____

Additional Notes: _____

Running Totals: Physical-   Mental/Psychological-   Tactical-

The Soccer Training Journal: The Player's Guide to Daily Excellence

Day 54

"Perfection is not attainable, but if we chase perfection we can catch excellence." -Vince Lombardi

<u>Time Invested</u>   <u>Component</u>   <u>What you did</u>

        Physical Game: _____

_____

_____

        Psychological/Mental Game: _____

_____

_____

        Tactical Game: _____

_____

_____

Nutrition

Food: _____

_____

_____

Water: _____

_____

What did you learn today?_____

_____

Did you accomplish your goal today?_____

_____

What is your goal for tomorrow? _____

_____

Additional Notes: _____

Running Totals: Physical-   Mental/Psychological-   Tactical-

The Soccer Training Journal: The Player's Guide to Daily Excellence

Day 55

"If it doesn't challenge you, it doesn't change you." -Fred Devito

<u>Time Invested</u>   <u>Component</u>   <u>What you did</u>

        Physical Game: _____

_____

_____

        Psychological/Mental Game: _____

_____

_____

        Tactical Game: _____

_____

_____

Nutrition

Food: _____

_____

_____

Water: _____

_____

What did you learn today? _____

_____

Did you accomplish your goal today? _____

_____

What is your goal for tomorrow? _____

_____

Additional Notes: _____

Running Totals: Physical-   Mental/Psychological-   Tactical-

The Soccer Training Journal: The Player's Guide to Daily Excellence

Day 56

"Our greatest glory is not in never falling but in rising every time we fall."-Confucius

<u>Time Invested</u>   <u>Component</u>   <u>What you did</u>

       Physical Game: _____

_____

_____

       Psychological/Mental Game: _____

_____

_____

       Tactical Game: _____

_____

_____

Nutrition

Food: _____

_____

_____

Water: _____

_____

What did you learn today? _____

_____

Did you accomplish your goal today? _____

_____

What is your goal for tomorrow? _____

_____

Additional Notes: _____

Running Totals: Physical-   Mental/Psychological-   Tactical-

The Soccer Training Journal: The Player's Guide to Daily Excellence

Day 57

"It's a funny thing, the more I practice the luckier I get."-Arnold Palmer

<u>Time Invested</u>   <u>Component</u>   <u>What you did</u>

      Physical Game: _____

_____

_____

      Psychological/Mental Game: _____

_____

_____

      Tactical Game: _____

_____

_____

Nutrition

Food: _____

_____

_____

Water: _____

_____

What did you learn today?_____

_____

Did you accomplish your goal today?_____

_____

What is your goal for tomorrow? _____

_____

Additional Notes: _____

Running Totals: Physical-   Mental/Psychological-   Tactical-

The Soccer Training Journal: The Player's Guide to Daily Excellence

Day 58

"Happiness is not something you postpone for the future; it is something you design for the present."-Jim Rohn

<u>Time Invested</u> <u>Component</u> <u>What you did</u>

       Physical Game: _____

_____

_____

       Psychological/Mental Game: _____

_____

_____

       Tactical Game: _____

_____

_____

Nutrition

Food: _____

_____

_____

Water: _____

_____

What did you learn today? _____

_____

Did you accomplish your goal today? _____

_____

What is your goal for tomorrow? _____

_____

Additional Notes: _____

Running Totals: Physical-   Mental/Psychological-   Tactical-

The Soccer Training Journal: The Player's Guide to Daily Excellence

Day 59

"Start where you are. Use what you have. Do what you can." -Arthur Ashe

<u>Time Invested</u>   <u>Component</u>   <u>What you did</u>

Physical Game: _____

_____

_____

Psychological/Mental Game: _____

_____

_____

Tactical Game: _____

_____

_____

Nutrition

Food: _____

_____

_____

Water: _____

_____

What did you learn today? _____

_____

Did you accomplish your goal today? _____

_____

What is your goal for tomorrow? _____

_____

Additional Notes: _____

Running Totals: Physical-   Mental/Psychological-   Tactical-

The Soccer Training Journal: The Player's Guide to Daily Excellence

Day 60

"The quieter you become, the more you can hear." -Ram Dass

Time Invested   Component   What you did

    Physical Game: _____

_____

_____

    Psychological/Mental Game: _____

_____

_____

    Tactical Game: _____

_____

_____

Nutrition

Food: _____

_____

_____

Water: _____

_____

What did you learn today? _____

_____

Did you accomplish your goal today? _____

_____

What is your goal for tomorrow? _____

_____

Additional Notes: _____

Running Totals: Physical-   Mental/Psychological-   Tactical-

Fill This Page with Opportunities That You Have in Your Life

I have the opportunity to make a difference in others' lives each and every day.

Day 61

"You've got to be willing to lose everything to gain yourself." -Iyanla Vanzant

Time Invested   Component   What you did

        Physical Game: _____

_____

_____

        Psychological/Mental Game: _____

_____

_____

        Tactical Game: _____

_____

_____

Nutrition

Food: _____

_____

_____

Water: _____

_____

What did you learn today? _____

_____

Did you accomplish your goal today? _____

_____

What is your goal for tomorrow? _____

_____

Additional Notes: _____

Running Totals: Physical-   Mental/Psychological-   Tactical-

The Soccer Training Journal: The Player's Guide to Daily Excellence

Day 62

"There are no secrets to success. It is the result of preparation, hard work, and learning from failure."-Colin Powell

Time Invested   Component   What you did

    Physical Game: _____

_____

_____

    Psychological/Mental Game: _____

_____

_____

    Tactical Game: _____

_____

_____

Nutrition

Food: _____

_____

_____

Water: _____

_____

What did you learn today? _____

_____

Did you accomplish your goal today? _____

_____

What is your goal for tomorrow? _____

_____

Additional Notes: _____

Running Totals: Physical-   Mental/Psychological-   Tactical-

The Soccer Training Journal: The Player's Guide to Daily Excellence

Day 63

"Action is the foundational key to all success."-Pablo Picasso

<u>Time Invested</u> <u>Component</u> <u>What you did</u>

        Physical Game: _____

_____

_____

        Psychological/Mental Game: _____

_____

_____

        Tactical Game: _____

_____

_____

Nutrition

Food: _____

_____

_____

Water: _____

_____

What did you learn today?_____

_____

Did you accomplish your goal today?_____

_____

What is your goal for tomorrow? _____

_____

Additional Notes: _____

Running Totals: Physical-   Mental/Psychological-   Tactical-

Day 64

"What you do speaks so loudly that I cannot hear what you say."-Ralph Waldo Emerson

Time Invested   Component   What you did

    Physical Game: _____

_____

_____

    Psychological/Mental Game: _____

_____

_____

    Tactical Game: _____

_____

_____

Nutrition

Food: _____

_____

_____

Water: _____

_____

What did you learn today? _____

_____

Did you accomplish your goal today? _____

_____

What is your goal for tomorrow? _____

_____

Additional Notes: _____

Running Totals: Physical-   Mental/Psychological-   Tactical-

The Soccer Training Journal: The Player's Guide to Daily Excellence

Day 65

"Tough times never last, but tough people do."-Dr. Robert Schuller

<u>Time Invested</u> <u>Component</u> <u>What you did</u>

      Physical Game: _____

_____

_____

      Psychological/Mental Game: _____

_____

_____

      Tactical Game: _____

_____

_____

Nutrition

Food: _____

_____

_____

Water: _____

_____

What did you learn today? _____

_____

Did you accomplish your goal today? _____

_____

What is your goal for tomorrow? _____

_____

Additional Notes: _____

Running Totals: Physical-   Mental/Psychological-   Tactical-

The Soccer Training Journal: The Player's Guide to Daily Excellence

Day 66

"Make each day your masterpiece." -John Wooden

Time Invested   Component   What you did

                  Physical Game: _____

                  Psychological/Mental Game: _____

                  Tactical Game: _____

Nutrition

Food: _____

Water: _____

What did you learn today? _____

Did you accomplish your goal today? _____

What is your goal for tomorrow? _____

Additional Notes: _____

Running Totals: Physical-   Mental/Psychological-   Tactical-

The Soccer Training Journal: The Player's Guide to Daily Excellence

Day 67

"The best dreams happen when you're awake." -Cherie Gilderbloom

Time Invested   Component   What you did

        Physical Game: _____

_____

_____

        Psychological/Mental Game: _____

_____

_____

        Tactical Game: _____

_____

_____

Nutrition

Food: _____

_____

_____

Water: _____

_____

What did you learn today? _____

_____

Did you accomplish your goal today? _____

_____

What is your goal for tomorrow? _____

_____

Additional Notes: _____

Running Totals: Physical-   Mental/Psychological-   Tactical-

The Soccer Training Journal: The Player's Guide to Daily Excellence

Day 68

"Believe and act as if it were impossible to fail." -Charles Kettering

Time Invested Component What you did

          Physical Game: _____

_____

_____

          Psychological/Mental Game: _____

_____

_____

          Tactical Game: _____

_____

_____

Nutrition

Food: _____

_____

_____

Water: _____

_____

What did you learn today? _____

_____

Did you accomplish your goal today? _____

_____

What is your goal for tomorrow? _____

_____

Additional Notes: _____

Running Totals: Physical-   Mental/Psychological-   Tactical-

The Soccer Training Journal: The Player's Guide to Daily Excellence

Day 69

"Don't count the days, make the days count."-Muhammad Ali

<u>Time Invested</u>   <u>Component</u>   <u>What you did</u>

        Physical Game: _____

_____

_____

        Psychological/Mental Game: _____

_____

_____

        Tactical Game: _____

_____

_____

Nutrition

Food: _____

_____

_____

Water: _____

_____

What did you learn today? _____

_____

Did you accomplish your goal today? _____

_____

What is your goal for tomorrow? _____

_____

Additional Notes: _____

Running Totals: Physical-   Mental/Psychological-   Tactical-

The Soccer Training Journal: The Player's Guide to Daily Excellence

Day 70

"You must not only aim right, but draw your bow with all your might." -Henry David Thoreau

<u>Time Invested</u>   <u>Component</u>   <u>What you did</u>

    Physical Game: _____

_____

_____

    Psychological/Mental Game: _____

_____

_____

    Tactical Game: _____

_____

_____

Nutrition

Food: _____

_____

_____

Water: _____

_____

What did you learn today? _____

_____

Did you accomplish your goal today? _____

_____

What is your goal for tomorrow? _____

_____

Additional Notes: _____

Running Totals: Physical-   Mental/Psychological-   Tactical-

The Soccer Training Journal: The Player's Guide to Daily Excellence

Day 71

"Every strike brings me closer to the next home run." -Babe Ruth

<u>Time Invested</u> <u>Component</u> <u>What you did</u>

        Physical Game: _____

_____

_____

        Psychological/Mental Game: _____

_____

_____

        Tactical Game: _____

_____

_____

Nutrition

Food: _____

_____

_____

Water: _____

_____

What did you learn today? _____

_____

Did you accomplish your goal today? _____

_____

What is your goal for tomorrow? _____

_____

Additional Notes: _____

Running Totals: Physical-   Mental/Psychological-   Tactical-

Day 72

"If there is no struggle, there is no progress."-Frederick Douglass

Time Invested   Component   What you did

      Physical Game: _____

_____

_____

      Psychological/Mental Game: _____

_____

_____

      Tactical Game: _____

_____

_____

Nutrition

Food: _____

_____

_____

Water: _____

_____

What did you learn today? _____

_____

Did you accomplish your goal today? _____

_____

What is your goal for tomorrow? _____

_____

Additional Notes: _____

Running Totals: Physical-   Mental/Psychological-   Tactical-

The Soccer Training Journal: The Player's Guide to Daily Excellence

Day 73

"To avoid criticism, do nothing, say nothing, be nothing." -Elbert Hubbard

<u>Time Invested</u> <u>Component</u> <u>What you did</u>

        Physical Game: _____

_____

_____

        Psychological/Mental Game: _____

_____

_____

        Tactical Game: _____

_____

_____

Nutrition

Food: _____

_____

_____

Water: _____

_____

What did you learn today? _____

_____

Did you accomplish your goal today? _____

_____

What is your goal for tomorrow? _____

_____

Additional Notes: _____

Running Totals: Physical-   Mental/Psychological-   Tactical-

The Soccer Training Journal: The Player's Guide to Daily Excellence

Day 74

"The more I want to get something done, the less I call it work." -Richard Bach

<u>Time Invested</u>   <u>Component</u>   <u>What you did</u>

Physical Game: _____

_____

_____

Psychological/Mental Game: _____

_____

_____

Tactical Game: _____

_____

_____

Nutrition

Food: _____

_____

_____

Water: _____

_____

What did you learn today? _____

_____

Did you accomplish your goal today? _____

_____

What is your goal for tomorrow? _____

_____

Additional Notes: _____

Running Totals: Physical-   Mental/Psychological-   Tactical-

The Soccer Training Journal: The Player's Guide to Daily Excellence

Day 75

"Your imagination is your preview of life's coming attractions." -Albert Einstein

Time Invested   Component   What you did

    Physical Game: _____

_____

_____

    Psychological/Mental Game: _____

_____

_____

    Tactical Game: _____

_____

_____

Nutrition

Food: _____

_____

_____

Water: _____

_____

What did you learn today?_____

_____

Did you accomplish your goal today?_____

_____

What is your goal for tomorrow? _____

_____

Additional Notes: _____

Running Totals: Physical-   Mental/Psychological-   Tactical-

The Soccer Training Journal: The Player's Guide to Daily Excellence

Fill This Page with Things You are Grateful for

I am a grateful for the opportunity to play soccer.

The Soccer Training Journal: The Player's Guide to Daily Excellence

Day 76

"The price of anything is the amount of life you exchange for it." -Henry David Thoreau

<u>Time Invested</u>   <u>Component</u>   <u>What you did</u>

      Physical Game: _____

_____

_____

      Psychological/Mental Game: _____

_____

_____

      Tactical Game: _____

_____

_____

Nutrition

Food: _____

_____

_____

Water: _____

_____

What did you learn today? _____

_____

Did you accomplish your goal today? _____

_____

What is your goal for tomorrow? _____

_____

Additional Notes: _____

Running Totals: Physical-   Mental/Psychological-   Tactical-

The Soccer Training Journal: The Player's Guide to Daily Excellence

Day 77

"There are no shortcuts to any place worth going."-Beverly Sills

<u>Time Invested</u>   <u>Component</u>   <u>What you did</u>

Physical Game: _____

_____

_____

Psychological/Mental Game: _____

_____

_____

Tactical Game: _____

_____

_____

Nutrition

Food: _____

_____

_____

Water: _____

_____

What did you learn today?_____

_____

Did you accomplish your goal today?_____

_____

What is your goal for tomorrow? _____

_____

Additional Notes: _____

Running Totals: Physical-   Mental/Psychological-   Tactical-

The Soccer Training Journal: The Player's Guide to Daily Excellence

Day 78

"If you can't outplay them, outwork them."-Ben Hogan

<u>Time Invested</u> <u>Component</u> <u>What you did</u>

        Physical Game: _____

_____

_____

        Psychological/Mental Game: _____

_____

_____

        Tactical Game: _____

_____

_____

Nutrition

Food: _____

_____

_____

Water: _____

_____

What did you learn today? _____

_____

Did you accomplish your goal today? _____

_____

What is your goal for tomorrow? _____

_____

Additional Notes: _____

Running Totals: Physical-   Mental/Psychological-   Tactical-

The Soccer Training Journal: The Player's Guide to Daily Excellence

Day 79

"The best way to predict the future is to invent it."-Alan Kay

Time Invested   Component   What you did

        Physical Game: _____

_____

_____

        Psychological/Mental Game: _____

_____

_____

        Tactical Game: _____

_____

_____

Nutrition

Food: _____

_____

_____

Water: _____

_____

What did you learn today? _____

_____

Did you accomplish your goal today? _____

_____

What is your goal for tomorrow? _____

_____

Additional Notes: _____

Running Totals: Physical-   Mental/Psychological-   Tactical-

The Soccer Training Journal: The Player's Guide to Daily Excellence

Day 80

"If you have everything under control, you're not moving fast enough." -Mario Andretti

<u>Time Invested</u> <u>Component</u> <u>What you did</u>

    Physical Game: _____

_____

_____

    Psychological/Mental Game: _____

_____

_____

    Tactical Game: _____

_____

_____

Nutrition

Food: _____

_____

_____

Water: _____

_____

What did you learn today? _____

_____

Did you accomplish your goal today? _____

_____

What is your goal for tomorrow? _____

_____

Additional Notes: _____

Running Totals: Physical-   Mental/Psychological-   Tactical-

Day 81

"Do not be anxious about tomorrow, for tomorrow will be anxious for itself. Let the day's own trouble be sufficient for the day."-Jesus

<u>Time Invested</u>   <u>Component</u>   <u>What you did</u>

Physical Game: _____

_____

_____

Psychological/Mental Game: _____

_____

_____

Tactical Game: _____

_____

_____

Nutrition

Food: _____

_____

_____

Water: _____

_____

What did you learn today? _____

_____

Did you accomplish your goal today? _____

_____

What is your goal for tomorrow? _____

_____

Additional Notes: _____

Running Totals: Physical-   Mental/Psychological-   Tactical-

The Soccer Training Journal: The Player's Guide to Daily Excellence

Day 82

"You never know how strong you are, until being strong is your only choice." -Bob Marley

<u>Time Invested</u>   <u>Component</u>   <u>What you did</u>

        Physical Game: _____

_____

_____

        Psychological/Mental Game: _____

_____

_____

        Tactical Game: _____

_____

_____

Nutrition

Food: _____

_____

_____

Water: _____

_____

What did you learn today? _____

_____

Did you accomplish your goal today? _____

_____

What is your goal for tomorrow? _____

_____

Additional Notes: _____

Running Totals: Physical-   Mental/Psychological-   Tactical-

Day 83

"Remember that sometimes not getting what you want is a wonderful stroke of luck." -Dalai Lama

Time Invested   Component   What you did

Physical Game: _____

_____

_____

Psychological/Mental Game: _____

_____

_____

Tactical Game: _____

_____

_____

Nutrition

Food: _____

_____

_____

Water: _____

_____

What did you learn today? _____

_____

Did you accomplish your goal today? _____

_____

What is your goal for tomorrow? _____

_____

Additional Notes: _____

Running Totals: Physical-   Mental/Psychological-   Tactical-

The Soccer Training Journal: The Player's Guide to Daily Excellence

Day 84

"Someone else's action should not determine your response."-Dalai Lama

<u>Time Invested</u> <u>Component</u> <u>What you did</u>

        Physical Game: _____

_____

_____

        Psychological/Mental Game: _____

_____

_____

        Tactical Game: _____

_____

_____

Nutrition

Food: _____

_____

_____

Water: _____

_____

What did you learn today?_____

_____

Did you accomplish your goal today?_____

_____

What is your goal for tomorrow? _____

_____

Additional Notes: _____

Running Totals: Physical-   Mental/Psychological-   Tactical-

The Soccer Training Journal: The Player's Guide to Daily Excellence

Day 85

"All we have to decide is what to do with the time that is given us." -J.R.R. Tolkien

<u>Time Invested</u>   <u>Component</u>   <u>What you did</u>

Physical Game: _____

_____

_____

Psychological/Mental Game: _____

_____

_____

Tactical Game: _____

_____

_____

Nutrition

Food: _____

_____

_____

Water: _____

_____

What did you learn today? _____

_____

Did you accomplish your goal today? _____

_____

What is your goal for tomorrow? _____

_____

Additional Notes: _____

Running Totals: Physical-   Mental/Psychological-   Tactical-

Day 86

"Let's not just reach for the stars, but become the stars everyone reaches for." -Robbie Kwia

Time Invested   Component   What you did

        Physical Game: _____

_____

_____

        Psychological/Mental Game: _____

_____

_____

        Tactical Game: _____

_____

_____

Nutrition

Food: _____

_____

_____

Water: _____

_____

What did you learn today? _____

_____

Did you accomplish your goal today? _____

_____

What is your goal for tomorrow? _____

_____

Additional Notes: _____

Running Totals: Physical-   Mental/Psychological-   Tactical-

The Soccer Training Journal: The Player's Guide to Daily Excellence

Day 87

"We often forget to draw a new picture because we are so busy criticizing others paintings."- Debasish Mridha

Time Invested   Component   What you did

Physical Game: _____

_____

_____

Psychological/Mental Game: _____

_____

_____

Tactical Game: _____

_____

_____

Nutrition

Food: _____

_____

_____

Water: _____

_____

What did you learn today? _____

_____

Did you accomplish your goal today? _____

_____

What is your goal for tomorrow? _____

_____

Additional Notes: _____

Running Totals: Physical-   Mental/Psychological-   Tactical-

The Soccer Training Journal: The Player's Guide to Daily Excellence

Day 88

"Find the good, and praise it."-Alex Haley

<u>Time Invested</u> <u>Component</u> <u>What you did</u>

    Physical Game: _____

_____

_____

    Psychological/Mental Game: _____

_____

_____

    Tactical Game: _____

_____

_____

Nutrition

Food: _____

_____

_____

Water: _____

_____

What did you learn today? _____

_____

Did you accomplish your goal today? _____

_____

What is your goal for tomorrow? _____

_____

Additional Notes: _____

Running Totals: Physical-   Mental/Psychological-   Tactical-

The Soccer Training Journal: The Player's Guide to Daily Excellence

Day 89

"In the middle of every difficulty lies opportunity." -Albert Einstein

<u>Time Invested</u>   <u>Component</u>   <u>What you did</u>

    Physical Game: _____

_____

_____

    Psychological/Mental Game: _____

_____

_____

    Tactical Game: _____

_____

_____

Nutrition

Food: _____

_____

Water: _____

_____

What did you learn today? _____

_____

Did you accomplish your goal today? _____

_____

What is your goal for tomorrow? _____

_____

Additional Notes: _____

Running Totals: Physical-   Mental/Psychological-   Tactical-

The Soccer Training Journal: The Player's Guide to Daily Excellence

Day 90

"How wonderful it is that nobody need wait a single moment before starting to improve the world."-Anne Frank

<u>Time Invested</u> <u>Component</u> <u>What you did</u>

     Physical Game: _____

_____

_____

     Psychological/Mental Game: _____

_____

_____

     Tactical Game: _____

_____

_____

Nutrition

Food: _____

_____

_____

Water: _____

_____

What did you learn today? _____

_____

Did you accomplish your goal today? _____

_____

What is your goal for tomorrow? _____

_____

Additional Notes: _____

Running Totals: Physical-   Mental/Psychological-   Tactical-

The Soccer Training Journal: The Player's Guide to Daily Excellence

Fill This Page with a Thank You Letter to Yourself for How Much You Have Committed Yourself to Making Your Dreams Come True This Season

Recognizing Our Accomplishments

"Who seeks shall find."-Sophocles

Time Invested in My:

Physical Game- _____

Psychological/Mental Game- _____

Tactical Game- _____

Total Game _____

The number of times I accomplished my goal for the day: _____

Most important things that I learned this season: _____
_____
_____

Most challenging situation this season: _____
_____
_____

Greatest personal accomplishment this season: _____
_____
_____

Greatest team accomplishment this season: _____
_____
_____

Additional Notes on This Season: _____
_____
_____

What Do I Do Next?

Congratulations on completing 90 days in your soccer journey! On the following page, you will set goals for next season. As you look forward to the future, take a look back at this past season. On the previous page, you took the opportunity to recognize your accomplishments from this past season. Did you accomplish all of your goals? Were you as physically and mentally as strong as you would have liked to be? Did you make the best decisions in game situations? Have you become the player that you would love to watch on the television?

When you think about these questions, look at how much time you invested in your physical game, psychological/mental game, tactical game, and total game. Were your strongest abilities a product of additional training in your physical, psychological/mental, or tactical game? If a component of your game could use improvement, this should be your first focus for your next season. The more strengths you develop in your game through challenging yourself in training that skill, the more prepared you become for the next level of the game.

Once you have completed the "Preparing for Next Season" page that follows, consider purchasing another copy of *The Soccer Training Journal: The Player's Guide to Daily Excellence*. This is a great way to track your progress over time. As you mark your age, weight, height, league, and the starting date at the beginning of each journal, it is serves as a sort of soccer time machine. As you go through the highs and lows of development in sport, you can look back on previous seasons and even specific days where you actualized your greatest successes. In doing this, you will be able to recognize what has worked best for you in the past and plan for the future. A great player is consistent in their habits and is courageous enough to train their weaknesses into strengths. Here's to future successes in soccer!

The Soccer Training Journal: The Player's Guide to Daily Excellence

Preparing for Next Season

"Arriving at one goal is the starting point to another." -John Dewey

Life Goal in Soccer: _____

_____

Season Goal in Soccer: _____

_____

Favorite Player(s): _____

_____

_____

Favorite Skill(s): _____

_____

_____

Best Personal Soccer Attribute(s): _____

_____
_____
_____
_____

References

Mitchell, H. H., Hamilton, T. S., Steggerda, F. R., & Bean, H. W. (1945). The chemical composition of the adult human body and its bearing on the biochemistry of growth. *Journal of Biological Chemistry, 168*, 625-637.

About the Author

Brad Gieske has always had a passion for soccer. Growing up, he played on Missouri's Olympic Development Program team, was co-captain for a back-to-back state championship soccer team at St. Dominic, and was part of the training squad for a semi-professional team at the age of 17 years.

After suffering illness that made him too weak to continue his collegiate soccer career, Brad came back to his home town to start his career as a soccer coach. Shortly after returning home, he became President of Jogadores Soccer Club; became certified as a personal trainer; became the in-house soccer trainer for a local futsal facility; earned a degree in Exercise Science with minors in Chemistry and Nutrition; co-founded a physical education company named Project-TAG with sport psychologist and former Olympic coach, Paul Wright; and began work for SoccerPlus, founded by former World Cup- and Olympic gold-winning United States Women's National Team coach Tony DiCicco, as a staff coach.

Now, Brad works as a full-time employee at Lindenwood University's Sport Science Center, operating as a researcher in the areas of exercise and nutrition while completing his Master's degree in Human Performance; runs Jogadores soccer club; promotes Project-TAG to physical education teachers, coaches, and players; goes on medical and soccer outreach programs, most recently to Kenya for one month and Haiti in the near future, to provide love and support for the people of the world through "the beautiful game;" and trains hundreds of players each year in the pursuit of passing on all of the great lessons and opportunities that soccer provides a player who loves the game.

In the near future, he will work as manager of soccer operations for Lax Hut Village, continue pursuing opportunities to travel and provide soccer outreach around the world, and will continue his education on and off of the field.

Made in the USA
Middletown, DE
23 January 2017